All Families
Military Families

by Connor Stratton

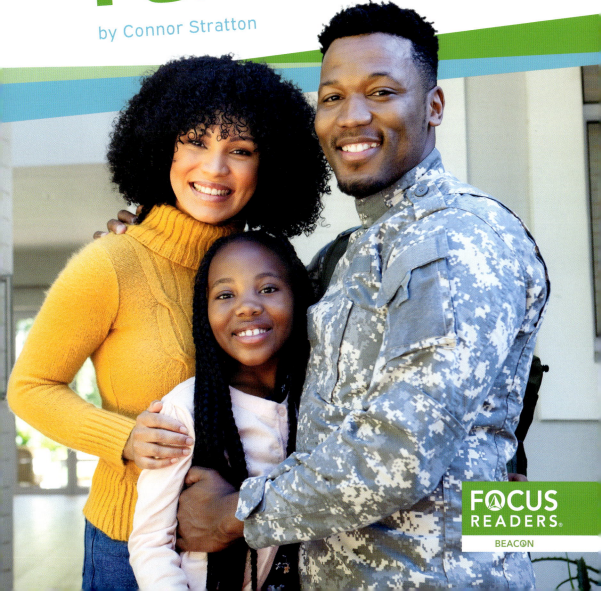

FOCUS READERS®
BEACON

www.focusreaders.com

Copyright © 2025 by Focus Readers®, Mendota Heights, MN 55120. All rights reserved. No part of this book may be reproduced or utilized in any form or by any means without written permission from the publisher.

Focus Readers is distributed by North Star Editions:
sales@northstareditions.com | 888-417-0195

Produced for Focus Readers by Red Line Editorial.

Photographs ©: Shutterstock Images, cover, 1, 8, 14, 17, 19, 25, 27, 29; Cpl. Henry Rodriguez II/US Marine Corps/DVIDS, 4; Senior Airman Alexis Orozco/US Air Force/DVIDS, 7; Tech. Sgt. Sarah Corrice/US Air Force/DVIDS, 10; Cpl. Matthew DeVirgilio/US Army/DVIDS, 13; Corey Toye/US Army/DVIDS, 20–21; Ilka Cole/US Air Force/DVIDS, 22

Library of Congress Cataloging-in-Publication Data
Names: Stratton, Connor, author.
Title: Military families / by Connor Stratton.
Description: Mendota Heights, MN: Focus Readers, Beacon, 2025. | Series: All families | Includes index. | Audience: Grades 2-3
Identifiers: LCCN 2024027405 (print) | LCCN 2024027406 (ebook) | ISBN 9798889983927 (hardcover) | ISBN 9798889984207 (paperback) | ISBN 9798889984757 (pdf) | ISBN 9798889984481 (ebook)
Subjects: LCSH: Children of military personnel--United States--Juvenile literature. | Families of military personnel--United States--Juvenile literature. | United States--Armed Forces--Military life--Juvenile literature.
Classification: LCC UB403 .S774 2025 (print) | LCC UB403 (ebook) | DDC 355.1/20973--dc23/eng/20240702
LC record available at https://lccn.loc.gov/2024027405
LC ebook record available at https://lccn.loc.gov/2024027406

Printed in the United States of America
Mankato, MN
012025

About the Author

Connor Stratton writes and edits nonfiction children's books. He lives in Minnesota.

Table of Contents

CHAPTER 1
Welcome Home 5

CHAPTER 2
About Military Families 9

CHAPTER 3
Challenges 15

 MANY IDENTITIES
Disabilities 20

CHAPTER 4
Dealing with Challenges 23

Focus on Military Families • 28
Glossary • 30
To Learn More • 31
Index • 32

Chapter 1

Welcome Home

A boy is feeling many emotions. His mother is coming home today. She has been **deployed** for seven months. She was on a **tour** in the US Army.

Family members often bring signs and balloons when their loved ones return.

The boy's family goes to the military **base**. They enter a massive building. Many other families are there, too.

Soon, huge doors open. A group of soldiers walk through. The boy sees his mom! He runs over to her. The boy gives his mom a big hug. He missed her so much. He was

Did You Know?

Tours often last six months to a year. But they can be shorter or longer.

 Kids often feel lots of different emotions when their parents return from a tour.

worried about her. The boy also feels nervous. He doesn't know what life at home will be like. Most of all, the boy feels happy. His mom is finally back home.

Chapter 2

About Military Families

In a military family, at least one parent is a member of the military. Sometimes, two parents are. Some military parents are soldiers. There are many other military jobs, too.

 Having a parent in the military can be a big source of pride.

 Bases sometimes have activities for children of military members.

Military bases can be a large part of families' lives. Bases are similar to large towns. They have stores and hospitals. Some have schools. Most families do not live on the base. But they often live nearby. And some families do live on the base.

The lives of military families have two different parts. One is when the military parent is at the base. Then, life can be similar to non-military families. Parents go to work during the day. They come home around dinner time. Children can spend time with their parents during this period.

The second part is deployment. The military sends the parent on a tour. The parent leaves home. The parent may go to another country. Some parents take part in **combat**.

Military parents come home after their deployments. But many parents do more than one tour. If they do, the family moves. They go

More than 1.6 million US children are in military families.

 It can be hard for kids to know that their parents are in war zones.

to a new base. Military parents get ready there. They train for the next deployment. Most military families move every two to three years.

Chapter 3

Challenges

Moving every few years can be exciting for military families. For example, some military families travel around the world. They experience different **cultures** as a result.

 South Korea is one of many countries around the world with a US military base.

However, frequent moving is often hard for kids. For instance, it can be tough to form and keep friendships. Changing schools is another challenge. New homes are difficult, too. All of these changes can cause stress.

Deployment is especially hard for military families. Children miss

Did You Know?

Children in military families average six moves before the age of 18.

 It's okay to feel sad when a parent is away from home. Talking about it can often be helpful.

their deployed parents. Kids often feel sad and stressed. They may worry their parent will get hurt or die. As a result, children may have a hard time focusing.

17

Communication with deployed parents can be hard. There are often large differences in **time zones**. Meanwhile, home can feel like a single-parent family. The parent at home has more responsibility. This parent sometimes struggles. When that happens, children notice. It can impact the kids, too.

Other challenges happen when military parents return home. Having them back can feel wonderful. But families have also

 Sometimes kids can talk to military parents using computers or smartphones.

gotten used to the parent not being home. Routines shift. Roles shift, too. These changes are sometimes stressful. It can be more intense the longer the parent was away.

MANY IDENTITIES

Disabilities

Military jobs can have risks. Parents can get injured in battle. They might see horrible things. These events can cause **trauma**. Parents may come home with **disabilities**.

Life is often harder with disabilities. For example, many buildings don't have ramps. They have only stairs. People who use wheelchairs cannot go there. Also, some jobs don't adjust enough for disabilities. So, disabled parents may not be able to work. Health care can be costly, too. Then families may not have enough money. All family members can be impacted.

Approximately one in five kids in military families have a parent with a disability.

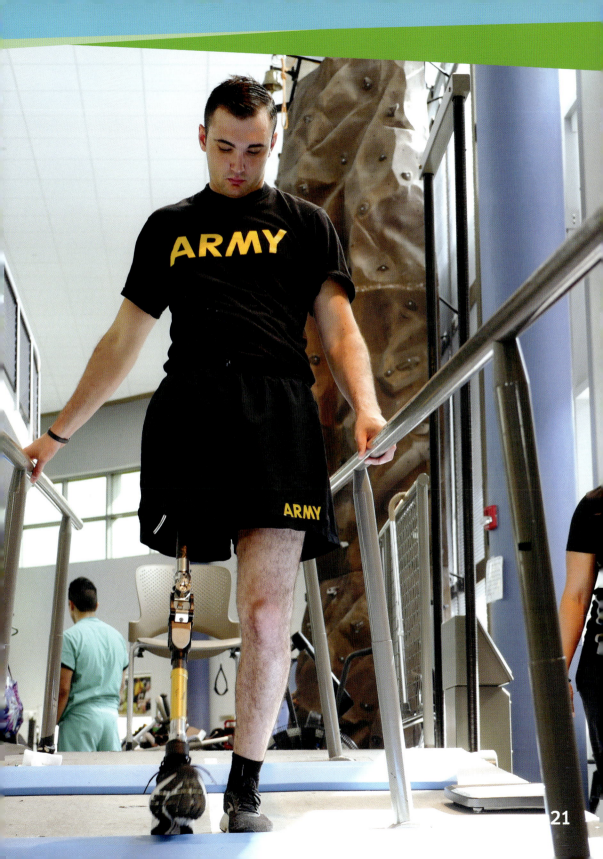

Chapter 4

Dealing with Challenges

The challenges of military families can be hard. But there are ways to make them easier. It's often helpful to meet other kids in military families. They already understand what it's like.

 Being around other military kids can make life feel more normal.

23

Communication with family members can also help. Suppose a parent is coming home after a deployment. Family members can talk about the transition. They can discuss what routines might change. They can share how those changes might feel. Families can talk through ideas to help.

Many places have programs for military families. Workers help families process their experiences. They provide other support, too.

 After a military parent returns, there are often good and bad changes.

Moving often can be hard. Kids may close themselves off to others. For example, losing close friends is painful. So, some children may not let friends form close bonds.

That way, it feels less painful during the next move. Even so, kids still feel big emotions. Being closed off can make it harder to deal with those feelings.

Friends and classmates can help. They can be kind. They can work to

Did You Know?

Many military children develop resilience. They learn how to deal with tough events. Then new challenges feel less scary.

 Having someone to talk to can make life feel easier during hard times.

understand what it's like moving a lot. Or they can show kids around the school or neighborhood. These actions may make the move easier.

FOCUS ON Military Families

Write your answers on a separate piece of paper.

1. Write a paragraph explaining the main ideas of Chapter 2.

2. Would you ever want to join the military? Why or why not?

3. How often do most military families move?
    - A. every two months
    - B. every two to three years
    - C. every 20 years

4. Why would being in a different time zone make communication hard?
    - A. Family members are not awake at the same time.
    - B. Phones only work within one time zone.
    - C. Families are never allowed to talk to deployed parents.

5. What does **transition** mean in this book?

*Family members can talk about the **transition**. They can discuss what routines might change.*

    A. a shift
    B. a routine
    C. a family

6. What does **resilience** mean in this book?

*Many military children develop **resilience**. They learn how to deal with tough events. Then new challenges feel less scary.*

    A. an ability to scare other people away
    B. an ability to stop hard things from happening
    C. an ability to get better after a difficult event

Answer key on page 32.

Glossary

base
A place where military supplies are kept and where members of the military train.

combat
Fighting between armed forces.

cultures
Groups of people and the ways they live, including their customs, beliefs, and laws.

deployed
Called into military action.

disabilities
Conditions of the body or mind that make it harder for a person to do certain activities.

time zone
An area where one time is used by everybody.

tour
A stretch of time when someone in the military works in a certain place. A tour usually happens away from home.

trauma
A feeling of lasting fear and shock after a difficult experience.

To Learn More

BOOKS

Johnson, Chelsea, LaToya Council, and Carolyn Choi. *Love Without Bounds: An IntersectionAllies Book About Families*. New York: Dottir Press, 2023.

Murray, Julie. *My Military Parent*. Minneapolis: Abdo Publishing, 2021.

Pearl, Melissa Sherman, and David A. Sherman. *Making a Difference with Cell Phones for Soldiers*. Ann Arbor, MI: Cherry Lake Publishing, 2024.

NOTE TO EDUCATORS

Visit **www.focusreaders.com** to find lesson plans, activities, links, and other resources related to this title.

Index

B
bases, 6, 10 – 11, 13

C
combat, 12
communication, 18, 24
cultures, 15

D
deployment, 5, 12–13, 16–18, 24
disabilities, 20

F
friends, 16, 25–26

M
moving, 12–13, 15–16, 25–27

P
programs, 24

R
resilience, 26
routines, 19, 24

S
school, 11, 16, 27
soldiers, 6, 9
stress, 16–17, 19

T
tours, 5–6, 12
training, 13
trauma 20

Answer Key: 1. Answers will vary; **2.** Answers will vary; **3.** B; **4.** A; **5.** A; **6.** C